A COLLECTION OF POEMS

By

William R. Holmes

Publisher's Name: William R. Holmes

ISBN: 978-1-962142-57-1

CONTENTS

A FRIEND'S GOODBYE

So long my friend today I am sad
cherished memories, the great times we had
in my mind I can still see you, beautifully clad
your smiling face that always made me glad
we were confidantes, discussed the good and the bad
such youth and vitality, kept me giddy and feeling like a lad
truly it has been meaningful, this friendship was no fad
shall I miss you, oh I guess I will miss you just a tad
reality is, the loss is a misery, so once again let me add
forever in my heart but now gone, and today I am sad

A GRANDMOTHER'S LOVE

What cherished memories, the unselfish love that was constantly showed,
An image of womanhood, the proper behaviors and ideals you nobly bestowed.
Those crisp mornings, you were never too busy to play the host,
A satisfying breakfast awaits, of eggs, grits, bacon, and toast.

The scrumptious meals you prepared, to your family and friends were always a delight,
Hours in the kitchen, the baking flour was everywhere, the room seemed blanketed in white.
But cleaning up was no worry, the empty plates and gratified palates made your heart smile,
Then everyone out to the front porch, to sit, relax, and chat for awhile.

The house was a home, no mansion or any other abode could aptly compare,
Upon entering warmth was felt, few ever experienced a more welcoming existence, while they were there.
Life could be very trying, anxiety and pain were a part of many of your days,
But strength and dignity won, and love continuously shone through in so many ways.

Many years have passed, but I'm constantly reminded of the influence you had in my life,
The blessing of family, the respect and love that I am daily shown from my son and my wife.
But there's no love like a Grandmother's, and your absence makes me sad and brings a tear to the eye,
However I'm comforted by God's promise that again we'll be together, in the sweet bye and bye.

A Summer Day on Buffalo Bayou

The sun rises early, this day will prove to be hot,
Often the rustling of the natives can be heard, today they were not.
The gentle flow of the water, it barely makes a sound,
The crawly creatures avoid the daylight, so none can be found.

Step stones for a pathway, grass and weeds cover the ground,
The Cardinal departs his domain, while his Redbird awaits.
He's gone off to work, this noble protector of his mate,
The water is high, Kayakers enjoy the outdoors and the fun.

This peaceful activity in nature, under a blazing Texas sun,
Til dusk has appeared and darkness will soon follow.
The gentle humid breeze swirls around this place where we wallow,
Nightfall descends on this sliver of Texas soil.

On which generations have lived, labored, and toiled,
This waterway has a history, most proud, treasured, and true.
An enterprising highway of the past, as the populace and the cities grew,
Now an evening shrouded in darkness, one cannot hear a sound.

Except the feasting of the raccoons, as many abound,
The sight of the occasional Coyote comes into view
The night brings out the predators, the game they pursue,
Until it's time for the warm sunlight to shine once again.

Nature's finest creation, an estuary, a loyal companion, and friend,
Yet sadly marred by man, destined, one day, to transfer ownership
And return once more to the land.

CLOUDS

The cumulus gather, floating high, up in the sky Shrouding
a beautiful dome of blue
Ushers in a fine day anew
With a slight push from the wind, your journey begins
Hovering above the earth, as if stranded
Presence unnoticed, mostly taken for granted Seldom
credited for the tasks performed
When moisture reigns thine existence is scorned Tiny ice
droplets facilitate cool temperatures
Global safety at a cost, homospheric expenditures Oft the
personality darkens, danger abounds
Take heed and shelter, proceed underground
As seen from the heavens, a planetary beauty
A noble shade of color, doing its duty
A salute to our friend, the misty compages
May you remain with us always, and through the ages

FOLLOW THE PACK MENTALITY

A disturbance to the soul, to be omitted from the group
The things that must be missed if one is not in the loop
Group think becomes a contagion that swells as each day passes
As the message of fear and intimidation are ushered to the masses
A sad state of affairs when one questions the validity of their own thoughts
Oh wayward traveler what treachery and sinfulness you have wrought
Away with your archaic ideals, dismiss all that you have been taught
The new message, the new truth, ignore the awful misery that you see
Should there be any questions, the answers are provided, just listen to me
All will be adherents, the influencers have such devotees, so they must be right
Their information highways operate on schedule, all during the day and night
Ever posting and tweeting, impossible to escape, try as one might
Inevitably the weakened are worn down and agree, tragically, to follow
Transformed into an automaton, now pitifully soulless and hollow

FRIENDSHIPS

It is said that to have a friend one must be a friend
On this I have to wonder, when these days it seems
That honor, caring, and relationships are totally thrown asunder
How can it be that so much time is spent trying to nurture a soul
Yet time and again we're set adrift, oh lord it takes its toll
Humans are a social sort, on this we aren't confused
But over and over we're left in pain, we're only being used
Take heart fellow life traveler, don't abandon hope
There are still those in need
And if we pray, and search each day, we'll find a friend indeed.

GETTING THE GOLD

Let's sell our soul
We must go get the Gold
Regardless of what it takes
Total disregard for consequences or mistakes
Be smart, be decisive, and be bold
The road to happiness is for those who go for the gold
Honesty, hard work, sincerity, and integrity?
Old worn out clichés for the average, as the wise see limitless prosperity
Do what is required, the ends justifies the means
Nothing can abate these endless, insatiable monetary dreams
To obtain the status, to raise the station requires riches untold
So to be influential and consequential better go for the gold
Only one thing matters, be delivered from principles
To whomever holds the gold their bad behaviors are permissible
What future lies ahead we shall see as the days unfold
Let us hope we don't lose our world as we could only be found going for the gold

HISTORY INSTRUCTS

What came before will surely come again
The past is a worthy guide
a lesson from a friend
Humankind possesses many habits
A favorite is making mistakes
Time and again events are revisited
The past is ignored and the same errors we make
Citizens of the world take heart
Study up on history and take the time to read
A tried and true road map has been provided
Worthy instruction on how to respond and to lead

HOW TINY WE ARE

How tiny we are, that live on this rock floating in space,
With our fast-paced lives, moving swiftly each day as if running a race.
How tiny we are, that reside in a galaxy two hundred light years in length,
Orbiting on our continual journey, a sun and a moon to give us strength.
How tiny we are, that our sun is a star, dwarfing the earth, key to our survival,
The Galactic neighborhood contains billions of stars, do we have a planetary rival?
How tiny we are, our God has chosen us, a speck of dust on a huge canvas,
Minutiae in an endless and timeless arena, a shimmer of light amongst the
blackness.
How tiny we are, yet could it be, that others dwell in the distant reaches?
Perhaps our heavenly Father demonstrates how special we are, that's what the
message teaches.

INSANITY RULES

We're on a ship of fools
where insanity rules
What once was good now is bad
The cloaks of resentment and anger now are clad
Follow the leader, a dastardly fraternity
To act otherwise is to eschew modernity
The popular and admired say what is best
Money and power is their ignoble quest
To become the new establishment is the goal wickedly sought
Utopian promises of communal delight and sustenance in every pot
There will be no dissimilarity of opinion, a refusal to debate
Cast the clouds of darkness that ensnare all of the hate
Violence and intimidation are the necessary tools
The manipulation has proven useful, the opposition are fools
Can a society exist in chaos, as these flags of treachery are unfurled?
Or is a conflict in store, to ultimately, from tyrannical hands, extricate the world?

La Grande Epoque du Baroque

L'époque Baroque, ce qui la rend unique,
Des styles multiples et audacieux, mis en pratique.
Avec un flair inégalé par tout autre,
Les dons multiculturels ne manquent pas, il a fait son entrée.

Ses doigts nobles ont touché toutes les facettes de la vie,
Une grande influence culturelle, nous avons vraiment été bénis.
Il suffit d'entendre la puissante musique du jour,
Les classiques de Vivaldi et Beethoven si impressionnants et purs.

Le théâtre et le design, suscitant des intérêts nouveaux et particuliers,
Appréciation accrue de l'art à la mode, sensibilisation culturelle éclairée et améliorée.
Le monde a gagné en vivant une telle période,
Combien cela nous a appris et influencé.

L'intérêt pour cette époque demeure, quelle chance pour notre monde cultivé.

LOVE OF COFFEE

Coffee, a revered, sought after, flavorful bean
The mere mention of its name, the excitement of caffeine
Our mornings begin bleary eyed, it's time for that first cup
No one speaks a word or utters a sound, we're not yet up
The percolator awaits, it shant wait for long
Grounds are poured in, the brew will be strong
Ah, the aroma, the smell of the coveted concoction fills the air
In sweet anticipation we wait, it's almost too much to bear
But in a flash it's done, the dark liquid is ready to be poured
This Go Juice is life, a fact , not to be ignored
Tis truly a drug, a dastardly addiction
Can't face the day without it, truly an affliction
There are no substitutes, this conviction one cannot swap
Because coffee is good, it's good to the last drop.

ODE TO A JOB

A job is a must for most on this we can't deny, too often it becomes a stressful chore

No matter how hard we try. It begins as an adventure, a salaried delight, as time goes on, we cease to belong

The activity becomes a fright. We go along to get along, we trudge from day to day.

With the tasks at hand, we make our stand and muddle through the fray.

With fresh morning smiles and greetings we attend the meetings, the weekly ritual we attest

And sit with wonder as our chieftain thunders, "we must strive to be the best!"

" we need more loans, OH, did I hear groans, on this there'll be no rest"!

With fluid dreams, we think of things like obtaining a new occupation

Then suddenly we awaken, we smell the bacon, we discern this must be almighty calling

We're in for life, accept the strife, don't let your star start falling

So be an adult, not a kid, tis wicked when we cry

With some endurance, we have assurance,

The role is ours, til the day we die.

OUR FRIEND KETO

A special thanks to our noble friend Keto
a lack of activity, the body turns to dough
The mid-section expands, cannot see our toes below the
mood becomes somber,the clothes we outgrow you're
heralded to the scene, vanquish the dastardly foe follow the
directions and a transition one will undergo dropping the
pounds, a new countenance is aglow
the feelings turn positive, a debt of gratitude we owe so thank
you again, for the slim figure we now can show

PEN IN THE INK

There's the possibility, we think, he's dippin' the pen in the company ink,
'Tis a tragedy when a man, so long in a profession, can allow himself to succumb.
His actions bestow, a lust to grow, the decisions made are dumb,
He's grouchy and mad, as if his heart is sad, until she comes around.

Then he springs to life, his voice cuts like a knife, the cheerfulness abounds,
Errors others make, in the mind of this elder rake, this *le femme* can do no wrong,

She has something to say, determined to have her way, dominance sways o'er the throngs,
No one risks idle chat, only to be smacked to the mat, it's safer to keep lips zipped

His Highness believes it's all about him, we're just bit players in his film, our piece of the rock has
been chipped, So let us play along, even though we know it's wrong, but there's nothing we can do
This lowly couple are having their day, but the good times aren't here to stay,
At some point, we'll bid them both adieu!

RAIN

Oh rain, how long must you remain?

You have been around for what seems like years

But actually it's only been days since you came

Your drops, from the heavens, how quickly they fall

Until the ground, saturated and shrouded in dampness

Leave us chilly and ill,prayers of sunshine are heard from us all

Precipitation nourishes the lands, thoroughly quenching the thirst before it's complete

Then the dark clouds, with the help of the almighty's hands, float gently away

Once again the earth rejoices in the sun's splendid glow, the warm rays we happily greet.

SATURDAYS GAME

Up at dawn, the big day rolls around

A sleepy yawn is the only sound

Clear the head and get energized, the day is long

Wearing the lucky jersey, so nothing can go wrong

Throw on the duds and roll, must go meet the crew

Down a few bevvies and socialize, Oh how time flew

The colorful throngs make their trek, the excitement grows

The venue at capacity, half filled with friends, half filled with foes

Cheer the squad to victory, the day has been won

There'll be more challenges to face, before the season is done.

Signed " Management"

Orders are to be obeyed,
My presence makes everyone afraid.
Anger me and you'll not get paid,
Signed, "Management."

I fly at fifty thousand feet,
Seldom venturing from the executive suite.
My world is an income statement and balance sheet,
Signed, "Management."

The Board of Directors are useful tools,
Quid pro quo to the letter, that's the basic rule.
I tell them what they want to hear, most of them are fools,
Signed, "Management."

Employees are a nuisance, most I do deplore,
They cry and moan, cause a ruckus, on this we can't ignore.
Once AI is developed, they'll see what I have in store,
Signed, "Management."

I'll stretch the truth—no, actually, will boldly lie,
Honesty is nice but hard to disclose, no matter how I try.
Transparency is just a word, for me it doesn't apply,
Signed, "Management."

Everyone respects me, a leader through and through,
They all want to be like me, a worthy goal to pursue.
But in reality, I can't relate, I haven't got a clue,
Signed, "Management."

Sir Baselcell Carcinoma

You're a *Ne'er-do-well*, Sir Baselcell, your presence is not wanted,
You appear so lucent, but this visit is a nuisance, upon the skin you've now flaunted.
The plan was to stay, you were never going away, unless forcefully removed,
So it's off to the physician, this is a serious condition, your efforts must be swiftly subdued.

Worse than an irritation, there is no limitation to the damage you seek to cause,
You appear to sputter, truth is you spread like warm butter, ever down deeper into the schnoz.
To the host, there is much sorrow, yet hope for tomorrow, as one feels the pain and burn,
Such a dastardly basalioma, Sir Baselcell Carcinoma, be banished and never return!

SOLO FLIGHT

A month has gone by since last had time to fly
Anxious feelings and nervous sensation
Have practiced only by flight simulation
Check out the bird, all is in order
Make no mistakes this game gives no quarter
Pilot in the left seat, instructor in the right
The temperature rises as the cockpit is tight
Put on the head set, the radio crackles
Beginning to taxi, we're back in the saddle
Push the toe break to center the runway
Maintain the center line, there is no going astray
The machine departs terra firma, upwind at takeoff speed
Checklist stationed on the lap, instructional words to follow and heed
Cruise the pattern and demonstrate skill
Nail the three point landing, "hey, you got the drill"
Now pull over and stop, the instructor departs
Two sounds can be heard, the roar of the engine, the pounding of the heart
Three times around the pattern, if appears that you are ready
Stay calm and collected, keep the mind clear and the hand steady
Up, up, and away, wow, you're flying alone
Deep down from within, new courage is sewn
Til finally the task is done, another exciting win for private aviation
Plane and pilot both in one piece, no minor cause for unreserved elation
So go and celebrate, the day's been a glorious success

A major step accomplished, true precision demonstrated at its best

The airman's life is noble, a fine art detailed to a infinite degree

Airborne and aloft in nature, untethered from basic life, soaring high and free

SUMMER

Oh the hot season is upon us, feel the balmy sun shine
The masses flock to the outdoors, the air like wine
Life seems to slow down a bit, the work life doth rests
The interest turns to life's pleasures, the vocation we temporarily divest
There's travel to the mountains, the cities, and the deep blue sea
Gives one time to recharge and reflect, perched upon the outdoor settee
The weather can be difficult to predict, on this, one must be forewarned
The mornings are sultry and pleasant,the afternoons facilitate storms
The sky grows dark, thunder and lightning erupt, the outdoor revelers take shelter
In any structure deemed safe and suitable, they huddle together
with a roar the rain falls heavily,provides the earth with a welcome respite
yet quickly the darkened clouds pass, surrendering to the heat in all its might
the land becomes greener, the foliage grows, the rivers and streams how they rise
the glow of the sun shines bright, and we get to view those beautiful clear blue skies
the season provides warmth for the soul and nourishment for life, nature at its best
to seek the seasonal adventures and all that is offered, yields the sense of being
powerfully blessed.

THE BALL CAP

The top of the head, occasionally hidden
Ill-mannered while indoors, strictly forbidden
Some old, some new, so many shapes and sizes
Emblems adorn, that no one recognizes!
Worn for sport and fashion
Becomes a habit,a peculiar passion
A closet full, quite a collection
Each has a story, a fond retrospection
Which one today, colorful or torn?
A few are pitiable, long left forlorn
Did you really buy this, what were you thinking?
It is ugly and plain, you must have been drinking
Noggin décor for every occasion and season
Wearers believe they are trendy, for some unknown reason
Therefore, the next time the notion strikes to don
Make every attempt to overcome, this distressing phenomenon
Keep the dome in view, avoid appearing crass
Leave the ragged nob covering at home, always strive to have class

The Dark Drink

The cocktail beaker adorns the bar, the alcohol cannot be far
Fill it halfway with cold clear ice, a garnish added to entice
Evenings are made for this, time to mellow
Relax and enjoy you lucky fellow
The contents are measured, a fine art of precision
Just the right amount, no improvision
The pouring proceeds, this noble libation
Smooth to the taste, a calming sensation
Savor the experience, perhaps have just one
Excess brings misery, and there goes the fun
For the spirits are for adults, up right and mature
Abuse is most shameful, and quite difficult to cure
Oh dark drink, an evening friend
A toast to thee, my glass I extend.

THE HANGOVER

Hit the town, time to socialize, sounds like a great idea
We must relax, join in the fun, all glory to the noble panacea
Proceed to the tavern, everyone is welcome, order up the rounds
But brother beware this can lead to real trouble, regardless of how pleasant it sounds
First one and then another, the juice of inebriation slowly takes hold
Until after a few hours the world looks different, you realize a bill of goods you've been sold
Return to the dwelling, fall into bed, the merry go round has captured the entire room
pay no attention, nothing is really spinning, the alcohol has simply sealed your cerebral doom
The sun arises to a brand new day however it is mid afternoon before you're awake
One longs for the shades to be drawn but the body won't respond, the whole anatomy aches
This will never be attempted again, another lessoned learned, it is always the same old story
Virtue is hard to pursue and temptation wins out until once again the poor soul becomes the
cocktail's quary

THE HUNGER PANG

Rushing through the day, one should not live life this way
Grab a morsel and it's out the door, cannot soothe the inner carnivore
Tasks to perform and much work to do, the midday meal we nobly eschew
the hours go by and the tank is empty, being task driven is the modus vivendi
the mind is weak and the stomach's in a knot, a friendly reminder, lest you forgot
til finally the end, the energy is gone, ignoring the inevitable and unable to prolong
how does one cope and continue to stand, the body needs nourishment and makes its demands
ill health is to follow, my friend please take heed, a well maintained temple is content, most contented indeed.

THE WAITING GAME

The Waiting game, what an awful thing
We spend half our lives awaiting an event
Do we really believe it's time well spent?
Hours become days, days turn to weeks, what anticipation...
If time does not soon yield a verdict our spirits will be shaken
Worrying accomplishes naught, it's vermin to the soul
What an ugly thing, causes rashes, wrinkles, and grayness, too soon to grow old
The only solution is patience, a soulful calmness to bear
Heed this noble virtue, meditate continuously in prayer.
For time belongs to no one, our time is not our own
This struggle is hard, oh how we hate the unknown
Remain sound, await on the outcome with a stoic, rational manner
Til moon and stars align and the universe reveals an answer.

TOUGH ON THE HOME FRONT

From morning until night, anxiety abounds

Constant worry and frustration, the anti-bliss makes it's rounds

Pick a subject and take the opposite approach

As time goes by, togetherness is a topic one dare not broach

Although there are moments that still bring joy

The real happiness is fleeting, too often all involved are only annoyed

Work at the office can be a challenge, but sadly many prefer the office to the home

With office work there's an end to drudgery, and one can enjoy just being alone

Basically, at the end of the day, the home is a business, a family corporation

The wise treats it as such, and gives maximum effort, as you're in for the duration

TRAGEDY FOR THE POPULACE

I

The sun rose brightly on that September morn
A busy day no time to waste, a new day is born
Fall is in the air with socials and gatherings planned
Excitement all around with high attendance in demand
Folks gathering together with much to drink and eat
Their coolers are packed with ice and a variety of meat
Then off to the grounds the facility of splendid delights
The smiles ofjoy and wonder extend will into the night
Until at last the weather beaten day must come to an end
How great it has been to be with both family and good friends
Yet it is time to travel homeward bound, exhausted and content
The darkness of night came quickly, scattering to the wind they went
Upon arrival, the mail has come bearing a most special invitation
The letter from an Uncle of the formal persuasion
It's always understood that such could occur, but on this occasion
The note is a request, which upon receipt, no hope of evasion
The Uncle has asked his nephews to attend the festivities
A unique set of tasks and skills, with life changing activities

II

Bags are packed but only basic essentials will be needed
Your presence is expected and prearrangements have been completed
An all day bus ride and the anticipation grows
A farewell to everyone, the sadness in their faces all show
No turning back, there is a duty and it shall be done
The spoils of victory favor the bold and the day must be won
At last the trip is complete, chaos is everywhere, running and shouting
The Uncle knows how to throw a gathering, Nephews abound, ever crowding
A humble abode awaits, complete with attire that is hopelessly too large
So much for so many, and everything is totally free of charge
Early to bed and early to rise, many sessions loaded into one day
The physical requirements are strenuous, endless running on that hard red clay
Lessons in the art of death and dismemberment, carrying the rod of steel
The education is enjoyable until it dawns on all, this soon will be all too real
The big day has arrived and the ten weeks has satisfactorily concluded
However, the Uncle now has another trip in store, all expenses included

III

A journey into the unknown, a life totally upended
Such a restless occasion, in a very strange world descended
The multitudes crowd the floor, many are arriving and many are leaving
What a basket of misery our new hosts are now weaving
Fresh faced new comers, carrying their bags
A mixture of fear and anticipation show on their faces
The departees experienced enough for a lifetime,
In hopes of never again to witness such places
Motoring over the terrain, what a bizarre foreign world
The existence is stark and bleak with its banners unfurled
Very soon the game will commence, this cadre of green men
Only twelve more months to go until this dangerous adventure will end
Every detail covered, each being thoroughly equipped for such hazardous business
But inwardly the shell is unfilled, the soul is unprepared for what the eyes must now witness

IV

Trudging along the pathways and through the damp weeds
Strange noises and sights, sweat pouring in the dreadfully extreme heat
Then the world explodes, the ground quakes and moves as loud as thunder
The devil has announced his presence and all the earth is thrown asunder
All the tools at his command, fire and debris rip up the spaces
Smoke and deafening noise surround this evil oasis
The dastardly perpetrators are totally unseen
Only the jarring of the sounds and the shrill of the screams
The fortunate find refuge hidden in the foliage and burrowed into the ground
The lost are sadly still, for they make not a sound
Fire from the explosions, splinters of devastation fills the air
Identify the foe's position and make a stand, but they seem to be everywhere
Then as suddenly as it began, the affront has ignobly ended
This worthless section of real estate has been bravely defended
Yet the consequences of the effort give tragedy it's due
The brave young faces that are now forever lost from our view
To those that survive, this event reoccurs with a constant and fearful repetition
Blood is spilled and carnage is wrought at this wasteful exhibition
Until at last, for the fortunate that endured, the lucky day arrives
Time to return to the world, to their hopes, their dreams and their lives

V

Civilization beckons once more, with hopes for a better tomorrow

For many there is no hope, as they dwell the loss with bitterness and sorrow

Few seem pleased to see the gallant returning lads, no well wishes, no job well done

For the average member of the societal club

There is little empathy for the hellish existence they've just come from

Injuries to the body and injuries to the soul, and what was the cost?

Lives destroyed never to see another day, with the angels they now dwell

The future of a nation and people perish, what good could they have done?

No one can tell

So many sons that will never bear children, start a business, run for office, or vote

The masses lament the loss, each engraved on a wall, the awe of their duty forever evoked

Yet the Uncle still makes demands, still extols the patriotic consciousness

So when Sam calls a gathering, a recipe could once more be in motion

For a tragedy of the populace

WEEKEND IN THE KITCHEN

Hey, What's Cookin?!
Let's SEE
We got meat, poultry, veggies, & fish
Don't forget the KETO, what a healthy dish
All the spices are ready so fire up the grill
Just smellin that aroma gives the neighbors a thrill
Fresh from the garden makes for splendid cuisine
Corn, okra, tomatoes, and those tasty green beans
For those who can't wait here's a bowl of Kale
Sit back and relax maybe have a cocktail
Can't wait, we're ready for the delight tonight
Because we love good cookin, It's dynamite

www.ingramcontent.com/pod-product-compliance
Lightning Source LLC
Chambersburg PA
CBHW061722120626
46550CB00003B/1323